Words of Praise For...

Stop Poisoning Your Marriage with These Common Beliefs

"This book is beyond common sense advice, it is excellent relationship therapy in a small, easy to read package."

—**Richard Rieman**, *Author,*
The Author's Guide to AudioBook Creation

"This book is incredible!! There is a mountain of quality content packed into this short format!!! Having done a considerable amount of relationship mentoring myself, I highly recommend this book to everyone in a relationship, looking for a relationship or having ever been in a relationship! This takes "demystifying" relationships to a whole new level. Bravo!"

—**Terri L. Wilber, CHt, CNLP,** *Program Director,*
Pacesetter Leadership Development, PSI Seminars, Denver

"Dr. Laurie Weiss and her husband Dr. Jonathan Weiss are truly experts in relationships and communication. Their insights are so right on. For anyone in relationship, married or not, this really looks at your underlying beliefs and how they shape your actions and reactions, and ultimately how that impacts your experience of love and the health and longevity of a relationship."

—**Philippa Burgess, Author,** *Inspiration and Ideals: Thoughts for Every Day*

"Too many couples start uncoupling from the get-go—giving up "joys" because the other partner doesn't like it. The reality that the Weiss' wisely layout in this "conversational" format is to let the one who enjoys continue to enjoy ... after all, it's insane to think that we are all clones. Refreshing. Realistic. Loved the short format."

—**Judith Briles,** *Author, How to Create a $1,000,000 Speech*

"My husband and I really enjoyed listening to the original recording of this book. It was very enlightening to learn about the different myths that we, as a couple, have fallen into. Shining the light on how we have behaved because of those beliefs helped us put a lot of our struggles into perspective. It also opened some great dialogue between us. I wish we had this information long ago; before we were married"

—**Lisa Mooney,** *Realtor*

STOP POISONING
YOUR MARRIAGE
with These Common Beliefs

The Secrets of Happy Relationships Series

DR. LAURIE WEISS

DR. JONATHAN B. WEISS

Empowerment Systems Books

Stop Poisoning Your Marriage with These Common Beliefs
A Conversation with Experts
The Secrets of Happy Relationships Series
by Dr. Laurie Weiss and Dr. Jonathan B. Weiss

The authors has done their best to present accurate and up-to-date information in this book, but they cannot guarantee that the information is correct or will suit your particular situation.

This book is sold with the understanding that the publisher and the author are not engaged in rendering any legal, medical or any other professional services. If expert assistance is required, the services of a competent professional should be sought.

First published by Empowerment Systems Books 2016 as Stop These Common Beliefs from Poisoning Your Marriage

ISBN (paperback) 978-1-949400-03-8
ISBN (ebook) 978-1-949400-04-5
ISBN (audio) 978-1-949400-05-2

Library of Congress Control Number: 2018907766

Books may be purchased in quantity by contacting the publisher directly at:
Empowerment Systems Books
506 West Davies Way
Littleton, CO 80120 USA
Phone 303.794.5379
LaurieWeiss@EmpowermenSystems.com
www.EmpowermentSystems.com

Cover: Nick Zelinger, www.NZGraphics.com
Interior Design: Istvan Szabo, Ifj.

Special Bonus

A VERY SPECIAL 60 MINUTE RECORDING

Our conversation with a group of
lay marriage counselors.

Little Known Secrets of Relationship Development
(MP3 Audio)

When you understand that relationships move through a
normal cycle of development, you are less likely to worry
about the natural and healthy changes you experience in
your marriage.

http://tinyurl.com/5cpqb4

Contents

Introduction

Interviewer: Hi, everyone. Welcome back to another quick read audiobook, **The Top Ten Hidden Beliefs About Relationships and How to Stop Them from Poisoning Your Marriage**, with Laurie Weiss Ph.D., and Jonathan B. Weiss Ph.D.

Relationship coaches and marriage counselors Doctors Jonathan and Laurie Weiss have spent over 40 years studying, practicing, and teaching relationship-building skills.

They are internationally known coaches, consultants, psychotherapists, speakers, and authors. They have presented their work throughout the United States and in 13 other countries.

Married since 1960, they have been in practice since 1972. They focus on helping clients create dynamic, effective, personal and working relationships.

Now doctors, what should the listeners' number one expectation or outcome be from this audiobook?

Jonathan: To realize that you have the power to create a fabulous relationship starting right now.

Interviewer: Excellent. Let's get started.

Chapter 1:
It Takes the Right Person

Interviewer: Hidden beliefs about relationships number one:

If you are with the right person the relationship will work. If it's not working, it must not be the right person. A relationship will only work with the right person.

What exactly is this and what should people do instead?

Laurie: It's actually the belief in soul mates that says there's only one right person out there for you. It's a belief that is wonderful at the beginning but it leads to disappointment, if not panic, when problems come up for the first time.

It may cause people to just decide this is the wrong person, it's time to end the relationship and never even learn to solve problems together.

Jonathan: I think what they need to do instead is to learn to focus on what's really important in the relationship and to talk about it.

Talk about what's desirable, what's truly a deal killer, what they want, and learn how to discuss and solve problems when they come up because they're going to come up. It happens in every relationship and it's not a sign of anything other than they are two different people.

Laurie: The thing is that soul mates are really a myth and every relationship has to be created.

If a marriage is going to last people have to learn the skills and be willing to deal with the kinds of feelings that come up that are not as happy as they were during the courtship.

Jonathan: If they don't do that they're going to get disillusioned, they're going to get angry at the partner for not being the perfect person they thought they were.

They will blame them, they wind up looking outside for somebody better, and they wind up being very vulnerable to having affairs or having serial marriages.

Interviewer: Tell me just a little bit more about this soul mate thing because that's actually something you read a lot about, you hear a lot about, especially on top psychology-type talk shows and things like that, people talk about their soul mate. What are people trying to accomplish with that?

Jonathan: It's kind of a nice, mystical, romantic idea that there's the perfect person. The truth is that every single person out there has flaws and has strong points, and anybody that you're reasonably attracted to, from our perspective, is somebody that you could work out a really good relationship with using relationship building skills.

Interviewer: Does this mean that, instead of saying that there's only one person out there, there's a certain type of person that is better suited for you than another?

Laurie: I would think that there are a whole variety of people. I wouldn't say that there's a certain type out there,

there's just a person that you might hit it off with some-where.

It might be somebody who's very much like you or it might be somebody whose needs and feelings are very compli-mentary to yours so that you can take care of them and they can take care of you.

I think one of the main beliefs that people have that gets in the way of marriage is the belief that we are all the same. We are not, we are very, very different.

If you think there's a soul mate, it means that we're already fixed, we're not going to grow, we're not going to change, we are the way we are, and we're perfect for each other. That just isn't true.

Very often people will get married and then what happens is, everything they thought about the other is wonderful, is there, but then something else will show up.

I was working with a client on the phone the other day. This was a second marriage. People generally don't come to us with this kind of problem when it's a first marriage, they just find another one. In the second marriage...

Interviewer: They try again?

Laurie: They find another partner instead of working it through with the first marriage.

Interviewer: Do they typically look for someone completely different than the first marriage or do they end up with someone who's very similar and just repeat the same mistakes?

Laurie: They repeat the same mistake. It's somebody who's wearing a different mask almost. They think, "Oh, this time it will be different. This time I've got the right one" but it doesn't turn out that way.

Jonathan: You have a bunch of criteria for what's going to be a good mate. When you start to form a relationship you're evaluating the other person, sort of testing them and seeing if they match your list, and that kind of thing.

That's a very different procedure and not a very helpful one compared to what can we create together? What is it that together we can do and create that is satisfying to both of us? It's different than testing them to see if they match your standard.

Interviewer: Okay, excellent. Anything else about this that we should be aware of?

Laurie: Well, my client who thought it was perfect, discovered it wasn't, called me when she discovered all the messes her husband had hidden in his closet, and then she worked out a way that she could help him clean up those messes instead of running, which was her first impulse.

Interviewer: So she decided to stay in there and actually work at it this time instead of cutting and running?

Laurie: [affirmative] Mm hmm.

Interviewer: Okay, excellent. Well, let's keep going.

Chapter 2:
Relationships Either Work
or They Don't

Interviewer: Hidden beliefs about relationships number two:

If a relationship is right, you shouldn't have to work at it.

What exactly is this mistake and what should people do instead?

Jonathan: Basically, what this mistake is, is taking each other for granted. You shouldn't have to work at it then that's just the way it is. You don't treat the person special the way you used to do, when you were courting, and trying to "win the relationship."

Okay, that's all handled, now we can just get back to a normal life. What happens when they do that is that the energy in the relationship, kind of dies out.

What they should do instead is deliberately pay attention to each other, catch each other doing things right, stroke each other. I know stroke is a technical word but pay attention to each other in an active kind of way.

Laurie: Everybody needs attention. Some people think, "Well, I should be able to give it to myself. I'm a grown up." That's almost like saying, "Once I eat, I've had enough food for the rest of my life."

We're biological creatures and we need to be recognized by other people in order to, actually to thrive, to live. There's a lot of information that says that animals and even people who are not stroked will eventually die.

Interviewer: What are some specific things that people could do or should consider when they're "working on the relationship"? Not in a way that, I guess a lot of times when people say, "I'm working on the relationship." It turns into this giant labor.

What would be some things to make sure you're paying attention to and are mindful of that would help you work on the relationship on a consistent basis and in a way that would really be beneficial to both of you?

Jonathan: There are some things that are so simple, it's almost embarrassing to talk about. Like, when you walk into a room or when your spouse walks into the room, to acknowledge their presence.

Laurie: To say "Hi."

Jonathan: To say "Hi," or as you walk by put your hand on their shoulder, tap them on the head. It's like a deliberate act that says, "I know you're here and that I like you being here."

Laurie: We're talking about positive attention. Very often what people do is pay attention to what's wrong and get into a pattern of telling the partner what's wrong.

In fact, I had a business client once who was so distracted he couldn't keep his mind on business because his relationship was in deep trouble.

He just couldn't get his wife to do the things he thought she should be doing and he would keep making suggestions to her. It just wouldn't work.

I gave him a very, very simple thing to do, which was to only talk to her for the next week about the things that she was doing right. That was all he did and he followed through.

The next time we met he was ready to go. His relationship was wonderful and he was thrilled about it. You'd be amazed at how something that simple makes a huge difference in a relationship.

Interviewer: That sounds like two really, even though they might sound obvious, they sound actually, quite powerful.

Jonathan: Yes.

Interviewer: Is there anything else to just give us the magic three? One is to acknowledge and one is to talk in the positive. What would be another one that would be just as powerful and actually pretty simple to implement?

Laurie: Because it's the physical.

Jonathan: Yes.

Laurie: It's remembering to hug each other. It's remembering to touch each other. Touch is the most powerful thing that you can do.

Jonathan: There's some research in a business context that says when the cashier gives you your change, if she touches your hand, puts it in your hand rather than putting it on the counter or dropping it in your hand, your opinion of the business and your loyalty to the business goes up.

Interviewer: Really?

Jonathan: It's as simple as that. Touch is very, very, very powerful.

Interviewer: Okay. Excellent. Well, anything else on this as far as things we can do to work on the relationship?

Laurie: I think that the most important thing is to remember that your partner is incredibly important to you and keep telling him or her that that is the fact.

Interviewer: Great advice. All right. Let's keep going.

Chapter 3:
You Should Know What I Want

Interviewer: Hidden beliefs about relationships number three:

If you really loved me, I wouldn't have to tell you what I want.

That sounds kind of familiar. What is this mistake exactly and what should people do instead?

Laurie: Oh, this is just an incredible thing that people to do each other. They say, "You should be able to read my mind. I've been looking all my life for somebody who could read my mind and I thought you were it."

Jonathan: Just like my mother, she knew what I wanted.

Laurie: Except she didn't really.

Interviewer: And you can't marry her.

Laurie: Right.

Jonathan: Lord knows we try, without thinking about it very clearly.

Interviewer: What's the advice for someone who hears that, and then what is the advice for someone who says that? Because I think we really have to address both sides of this issue.

Jonathan: Sure.

Laurie: Well, the advice for somebody who says that you should know what I want, should think about going into a restaurant with a waitress and saying, "Well, you should know what I want." And, the waitress just bringing what she thinks.

Instead of doing that, ask for what you want and you're much, much more likely to get it because most partners are quite happy to supply what's wanted. They just don't know what it is.

Jonathan: If you're on the receiving end of that, it's important to say, "You know, I care about what you want, but you know mind reading is a pretty inexact science.

You run the risk of my giving you what I think you want or even worse, what I would want if I were you. But I'm not you. I need to know what it is that you want and I'm very happy to provide it."

Interviewer: Okay, excellent. Any other thoughts on this particular issue? I mean, it sounds actually, pretty cut and dry.

You have to express what you want and you have to ask clearly for instructions on what is wanted. What happens if somebody digs in their heels? I've seen it, never experienced it myself, of course.

Jonathan: Yes, of course not, none of us have. We're always talking about finding...

Interviewer: Someone who you ask that to. Someone says, "You should just know." And you say, "Yes, I really don't know. I'm not a mind reader."

And they still persist. Is that, maybe, an indication that there's a deeper issue going on?

Jonathan: Well, yes. You know, some people really, if you dig, have the belief that it's somehow shameful or humiliating to expose what they want, to ask for it.

And some people are literally trained by their parents saying to kids in stores, "If you ask for it, you'll never get it. Quit asking me for things."

There's literally a training to not do that. You get that exposed if you dig into why are you so reluctant to ask for what you want. What's that about?

Interviewer: Okay, and if that is what you run into, any advice on what to do?

Laurie: The advice is to go back to think about how you were when you were a child. You asked for everything you wanted and you had to be taught not to.

You can go back and start doing that again. It's a natural part of being human to know what you want and to ask other people to pay attention to that.

Jonathan: To make demands of one sort or another. We are hard-wired to do that. We'd have to learn not to and anything that we learn we can unlearn, or we can change.

Laurie: Okay, excellent. Anything else on this, or should we move on?

Interviewer: I think we can move on.

Laurie: Okay, excellent.

Chapter 4:
We'll Always be In Love

Interviewer: Hidden beliefs about relationship number four:

Falling out of love means that the relationship is in trouble.

What exactly is this mistake and what should people do instead.

Jonathan: Well this belief shows up when ordinary life dampens the romantic high. The truth is that the bells-and-whistles stage of a relationship is a very early stage and it's only the first stage of a growing and loving relationship.

To think that that should be the entire relationship is like thinking that what goes on between a mother and a newborn infant is all there is to parenting, it's just the first stage so that's what the mistake is.

Did you want to add something Laurie?

Laurie: No relationships just naturally grow and change over time. They do go through predictable stages and we can help people with that, but we don't want people to blame themselves or each other or to try and capture the romance in order to have a truly loving relationship.

People think that being in love is all there is and they don't know the richness that develops into people who really love and accept each other warts and all.

Interviewer: Okay, excellent.

Jonathan: It takes a certain amount of energy and attention to move through the other stages of a relationship, to recognize what's happening and to talk about it and share the information.

There are some predictable changes that a relationship will go through. Having an idea of what those are and what they look like when they show up helps people put attention on them and get what they need as the relationship changes.

Instead they think that there's something wrong just because it's not as wonderful as it first was.

Interviewer: Yes, but if you're paying attention to what we talked about in hidden belief number 2, where you're actually working on the relationship then you're probably not going to experience this as much or you'll experience it in a way that won't feel detrimental, it will just create a topic of conversation.

Laurie: All of these beliefs reinforce each other, it's like looking at the same thing from different angles and really when people come to us about relationship problems what they usually say is, "We just can't communicate, we've got a problem communicating, we need to learn how to communicate."

When we look at that, it's ether a communication problem based on one of these beliefs where they are just stuck in the same rut or it's a problem that they simply don't have skills. Nobody has ever taught them that's it's possible to do things differently.

Interviewer: Okay, excellent. If somebody does find that they are stuck on this particular one, what advice would you give to get unstuck in this area or at least get things moving again in a positive communication direction?

Laurie: Well the first thing is to talk about it rather than to blame, to say "I'm not as excited, I need to think about what's important here, how do you feel?"

And to talk and to listen. In fact probably listening is one of the biggest skills that people don't develop before they deliberately learn how to do it.

Jonathan: Yes, a lot of what passes for conversation and communication is each person making their case and blaming the other one and then defending themselves against what the other one said, rather than actually sharing what's going on with each other.

Laurie: There's also something that they have to do which is give up believing in the magic because when you get married for the very first time and everything is bright and shiny, it's like believing in the tooth fairy and Santa Clause and the great pumpkin, you're going to live happily ever after.

Interviewer: Right.

Laurie: As soon as they find out that you're not going to live happily ever after, there's going to be some work involved in this, often quite a lot, they are just sad.

Jonathan: Disillusioned.

Interviewer: Whereas, if they concentrated on the payoff of that work which is a healthy, beneficial, wonderful relationship then …

Jonathan: Yes, and it's sometimes not just the payoff but actually the process of working together on it whether there's an outcome or not.

The process of working together to create something creates a much stronger bond because they're joined in making something happen.

Interviewer: Especially if you stick together through adversity.

Jonathan: Yes.

Laurie: Yes. One of the things that I've done is I've created a whole program about things that people can say to each other and talk about together to help them grow a relationship.

Interviewer: Oh excellent, where could people get more information about that?

Laurie: They can go to www.BeingHappyProgram.com.

Jonathan: It's an eBook that is actually direct instructions about how to have this kind of communication, how to structure it and what to say. It's in small chunks with weekly exercises.

Interviewer: Excellent, what's that URL again?

Jonathan: www.BeingHappyProgram.com.

Interviewer: Okay, well that sounds very helpful. People should go check that out. Okay, anything else about falling out of love means the relationship is in trouble?

Laurie: I don't think so, let's go on.

Jonathan: Yes.

Interviewer: Okay, let's keep going.

Chapter 5:
Act on Your Feelings

Interviewer: Hidden beliefs about relationships number five:

You should always act on your feelings.

What exactly is this mistake and what should people do instead?

Jonathan: This usually shows up in a typical pattern when a very emotional and bubbly kind of person marries somebody who's very controlled, quiet and stable.

The person who's emotional, in a sense, thinks that's what they're being hired for and they focus on their emotions and their feelings. They exclude logic and consequences and external limitations.

What you see is if they don't get their way they do temper tantrums, or hysteria, or they collapse. That's the exaggerated expression of emotion.

If one of them does it it's a battle, if both of them do it's a disaster. It can lead to all kinds of awful things; addiction, overspending, alcoholism, all kinds of stuff like that.

What they should do instead is learn to recognize that the feelings and the emotions are only one aspect of being a human being, and certainly only one aspect of a relationship.

It isn't that emotions don't count, it's that they're one of several things that count including what works, what doesn't work, what's the external reality, what does the other person think and feel. Those have to be included for them to learn to problem solve.

Laurie: Feelings are really, really important but they're signals that people need something. They're not directions that says you have to do something in a certain way in order to get that need met immediately.

That is something that people think is a way to behave. Somehow they've never learned that they can think about their feelings and they can talk about their feelings.

I think that is one of the most important things for them to learn.

Jonathan: Yes, if you think about it, somebody who's operating from an emotional position like that is operating sort of like a four-year-old (if you've ever seen a four-year-old meltdown).

Interviewer: Yes, I saw one of those about two hours ago.

Jonathan: It's charming in a certain way but it requires a grown-up to handle it. A grown-up relationship requires both people being grown up in order to actually handle it.

Laurie: Otherwise what happens in the relationship is there gets to be a struggle for control. One person gets to be under-responsible and flighty and the other one gets to be over-responsible and rigid.

Jonathan: Controlling.

Laurie: That may work out for a while but pretty soon the one who was controlling gets angry, or the one that is being controlled gets angry about it and there are uproars on both sides.

Jonathan: You can see how they trigger each other that way. The more controlling I get, the more emotional and reactive she gets; the more emotional and reactive she is, the more I want to control it.

Laurie: But then I might just be so tired of it that I start walking on eggshells. I don't say what I think and I don't say what I feel in order to avoid tripping up the other person and getting the out-of-control emotions.

Interviewer: If you find yourself getting into one of those downward spirals, either one, what do you do?

Laurie: Well, I've been working with a client lately who was blackmailing her husband by her emotional instability.

But finally what happened was ... she [realized she] was furious with him for trying to control her and telling her what was wrong with her.

She was thinking about what was wrong with him and not what was wrong with her.

What happened was she recognized how powerless she felt and that she was doing this. Really you need somebody to hold up a mirror for you so you can recognize it.

She began to see how her meltdowns contributed to the problem. She started gritting her teeth, at first, and not saying the things that were immediately coming to her mind, asking questions instead and listening. She was just delighted with how much power it gave her.

She's doing great now. She still feels emotional sometimes, but when she does, she talks about it rather than just expressing it immediately. He has calmed down and started showing his emotions. It's great.

Jonathan: One of the things that we have in the processes that we use with clients is a model that makes it clear to people, who don't otherwise think so, that they really have a choice about how to think, how to feel, and how to behave.

Most people do that automatically. They don't recognize that they can take a step back and decide to do something or not do something.

Somebody who throws a temper tantrum has a little moment before they do it where they say to themselves something like, "Okay, now."

If they learn to recognize that and step back from it, "What else could I do?" they could learn to control behavior that's producing bad results.

Interviewer: Okay, excellent. Anything else on this or should we move on?

Laurie: I think, let's go on.

Jonathan: I think we can move on.

Interviewer: Okay.

Chapter 6:
We Feel the Same Way
about Everything

Interviewer: Hidden beliefs about relationship number six:

My spouse and I feel the same way about everything.

Now why is this a mistake? And if it's a mistake or a wrong belief, what should people do instead?

Laurie: Well, remember what I said earlier, that they think everybody is the same, and my spouse and I are the same.

If everybody is the same then we don't bother to explore the richness in each other. What we do is we avoid having arguments.

39

Even if we have a hint that there's something different, we suppress ourselves in order to keep the peace and we pretend to agree. Then if we pretend to agree, eventually it wells up and one of us gets angry about it.

What people should do instead is recognize that everybody isn't the same.

I do this in businesses. Sometimes I give people personality tests and show them that they have different traits, just so that they get the idea that people are different, and need different things, and want different things, and that that is completely normal.

I tell them that when they come up with something that is different from their spouse, what they should do is say something like, "What I really am feeling right now is:

- I want to go for a walk by the river. And the reason I want to do this is I just need some peace and quiet,"

- "I'm tired of being so busy,"

- "I'm tired of doing the dishes,"

- Etc.

If the other person goes along with that, great. But if the other person, who hates walking by the river says, "Well, I'll come with you," it might be more helpful to say something like, "Are you really sure you want to go? It would be okay with me if you just stay at home. I'll be home in half an hour."

Jonathan: What happens when they don't talk about the disagreements is that the resentment builds up. They build up pressure internally and that's likely to break out at some future time.

I do what you want, I do what you want, I do what you want, I do what you want, and don't say anything about it. Finally I rebel, go out and get drunk, or some other extreme response.

Another thing is that if I comply with what you want when I disagree, and just don't say anything about it, my performance is likely to suffer.

I'm likely to forget and leave something out, or undercut what I said I was going to do because I really didn't want to do it in the first place.

Laurie: Like the businessman who retired and agreed with his wife that now that he was retired, he should do some of the housework. He just kept forgetting and he wouldn't do the things he said, but he tried.

Finally his wife got so mad one day that she kicked him out of the house.

He slept in his car and then he came to me in the morning. He was waiting outside my door. "What's wrong? What can I do instead?" We talked about it.

She came in a few days later and he started to tell her about the things he didn't want to do and those that he was willing to do. Things got a lot smoother very quickly.

Jonathan: I remember when we used to have an agreement that we would do stuff equally, and it'd be my turn to shop for the groceries when I really didn't want to go.

I discovered that I could go to the grocery store with a list, looking at it right in front of me, and come home without three things on the list, completely unconscious, but that was what happened instead of saying, "You know, I really don't want to do this."

By the way saying "I don't want to do this" doesn't necessarily mean I won't do it. But you need to give voice to it in order to clear that rebellious energy out of it. Does that make sense?

Interviewer: Yes, absolutely. It made me think that my wife and I just gravitated and then communicated about sharing the load. Each of us have different things that we do. We know that we are both doing things but we both feel like it's 50-50.

Jonathan: Yes, it used to be my job to clean out the cat box. About every three months I would surface and say, "Why is this always my job?"

Laurie would remind me why it's always my job, and she'd say all the things that were always her job and I'd think about it, "Okay, I'll keep cleaning out the cat box."

Laurie: When people are first married they do things that they decide don't work so well later on. Jon, why don't you tell them about what you used to do when we thought we agreed on everything?

Jonathan: Do I have any idea what you're talking about?

Laurie: The thing about the cameras.

Jonathan: Oh. I used to be very much into photography, and I still am, but I used to spend our discretionary income on camera equipment. You can never have too many lenses, stuff like that.

She didn't argue because after all I had this need and this desire and a very clear target. But she wound up getting very resentful that the discretionary money was being used up on my stuff.

Laurie: So one of the things that we came up with was we'd take the discretionary money and split it and each keep control over some of it.

That way I could have my share and save up for something big if I wanted to. I didn't need to impulsively spend it right away. It's worked out very, very well for the last about 48 years.

Jonathan: Yes, and I get to spend my money impulsively if I want to.

Interviewer: Well it sounds like definitely a good negotiation has taken place.

Jonathan: Yes.

Laurie: A long time ago.

Interviewer: But it sounds like the rules have stayed consistent which is probably important as well.

Jonathan: Yes, we found some rules that work for both of us and they're always open to renegotiation.

Interviewer: Excellent.

Chapter 7:
You Should Never
Hurt My Feelings

Interviewer: Hidden beliefs about relationships number seven:

"You should avoid hurting your partner's feelings in order to preserve your relationship."

Now, what exactly is this mistake, and what should people do instead?

Jonathan: There's a pretty deep assumption in here that's pretty common among people. Basically, it's that you're responsible for how the other person feels: that somehow we are responsible for each other's feelings.

We will talk a bit more about the other side of this in the next item, but this idea, that I make her feel so-and-so, really shows a lack of skill.

If I'm trying to avoid hurting her feelings, usually that means I have something I want to say or do that she isn't going to like. And if I think that I shouldn't make her feel bad, then I don't have any way of dealing with what it is that I want to do.

What I need to be able to do instead is get clear about what it is that I want, what I want to change, why I want to change it. And I need to learn to request the change that I want without blaming her or criticizing her for it.

"This is the way I would like it. This is why it's important to me. What's that about for you?"

Laurie: I think there's a possibility for confusion here because there's a very fine distinction about me responding to your feelings and you making me feel a certain way.

Sometimes, what happens is that I do react. I have an instant feeling response that isn't feeling good.

I don't like what just happened, but I don't have to stick with that. That's just how I feel at the moment, and one of the things that I need to be aware of, and that we help our clients become aware of, is that what I do with that initial feeling is entirely up to me.

You may be responsible for triggering the start of it, but I am completely responsible for how I continue to feel after it's happened.

Jonathan: Our saying is that, "Your feelings are a cow, but they're not a sacred cow." You don't like that I want to go up to Central City and play the slot machines for a day. That's how you feel about it.

Then we discuss what you want me to do or don't want me to do; and why that's important to what I want to do and don't want to do; and why that's important to me.

Laurie: One of the things that we tell our clients and each other is that, "You're not responsible for my feelings, but you are responsible for treating me with respect."

And "you are responsible for telling me about problems that come up, and I'm responsible for telling you about problems that come up for me." Because if we don't talk about them, they're very unlikely to go away by themselves.

Jonathan: Yes, and we wind up distancing from each other, and we then avoid hot topics and wind up walking on eggshells.

"I don't want to bring up this. I don't want to bring up that. I don't want to talk about that," doesn't make it go away. You wind up without any problem-solving about them.

Laurie: When this gets going, it turns into a really vicious cycle with couples. There was one where he was so afraid of setting her off, setting off her hurt feelings and making her unhappy, that he'd avoid spending as much time with her. He'd spend time at work instead.

Then, of course, the cycle was the unintended consequence that she felt hurt that he spent so much time away from her. And then she nit-picked, and exploded with her hurt feelings. That proved to him that he should stay away, and it just went round and round in circles.

Interviewer: How did they solve that issue?

Jonathan: This is a couple I was working with and basically, I was coaching him to learn to talk to her about the things that were troubling him without blaming her for them.

And that involved having to deliberately bring them up when they weren't already in the middle of an argument.

What he used to do was talk about those things but only after they were already fighting and in the middle of the fight.

Rather than raising it as a problem to be solved, he would throw that at her as a weapon to be used in the contest between them.

He learned not to do that and to initiate problem solving about them.

Interviewer: Okay. Excellent. Any specific advice for someone who either has their feelings hurt on a consistent basis or someone who finds themselves "hurting the other person's feelings" on a consistent basis? What should they do?

Laurie: Two different kinds of advice. For the person who finds herself or himself being hurt over and over again, the advice would be to think about what it is that's really important to you and tell your partner what that is.

And when you feel hurt, say, "I feel hurt, and here's why, and here's what I'd like instead."

Do you want to take the other side?

Jonathan: Yes.

Again, that involves being passive about saying that there's a problem. What needs to happen is the person needs to take initiative and say, "I'm aware I've been walking on eggshells around here, trying to avoid conflict.

And what that means is that we have some problems that haven't been worked out. Let's get them on the table and see what we can do to solve them, rather than my trying to avoid them all the time and making them worse by not dealing with it."

Interviewer: That's excellent advice.

Jonathan: A lot of it boils down to a very basic instruction, which is about open communication about what's going on.

Interviewer: Okay. Excellent. Anything else about avoiding hurting your partner's feelings that we need to be aware of?

Jonathan: Just really the reiteration. You're not responsible for your partner's feelings. You're responsible for your own actions.

Interviewer: Okay. Excellent. Let's keep going.

Chapter 8:
You Make Me Feel This Way

Interviewer: Hidden beliefs about relationships number eight:

My partner is responsible for how I feel.

Now what exactly is this mistake and what should people do instead?

Laurie: This is the opposite side of the mistake that we were talking about before. It's the belief that I'm not responsible for myself. It's somebody who keeps saying, "You make me feel."

What they should do instead is switch. Instead of saying, "You make me feel sad, scared," or whatever, is to say "'I feel" and "I feel mad, sad, glad, scared or ashamed, when you do this or when that happens."

Jonathan: I can think of a quick example that we've been into. Laurie used to say, "You're driving too fast."

Laurie: Now I say, "I'm scared," which is absolutely the truth.

Jonathan: Yes, I like driving in the mountains and I've been doing it forever and I know how, and I enjoy going fast in the mountains. She doesn't enjoy it so much.

Interviewer: I don't know that I would either, Jonathan. I'm just telling you.

Jonathan: Oh well, just don't ride with me.

Interviewer: Oh, nice. Okay.

Laurie: He usually slows down though when I say I'm scared.

Interviewer: That's interesting that you have a strategy for communicating that and it works. My wife likes to grab the console of the car and act like she's bracing for a crash. That's my cue that I need to slow down.

Jonathan: Does it work?

Interviewer: Oh, yes.

Jonathan: Oh, okay, good.

Interviewer: Yes. It annoys me, but …

Jonathan: Yes, non-verbal communication is just as powerful as words, sometimes more.

Interviewer: How do you deal with someone who thinks … Let's say you're in a relationship where again, let's give advice to either side of the coin.

What do you say to someone who really does feel like the other person is responsible? And what do you say to someone who is told that they're responsible and they know they're not?

Jonathan: For the person who thinks the other person is responsible, one of the things we focus on is to tell them that you're giving away your power.

You're saying the other person is entirely in control of your feelings and that you don't any ability or skill or responsibility for learning how to deal with your own feelings.

It's sort of like saying the other person has to do something about it if you have to go to the bathroom. It's something going on inside you. You need to learn how to manage.

Interviewer: That's a pretty powerful reframe right there. How effective is just that different perspective with most people?

Jonathan: You'd be surprised how startling it is.

There's some simple technology about how our emotions work that most people don't learn.

One of the things we typically don't learn is that there's something we can deliberately do about our own emotional state; that we can manage it in some way and that we get better results when we do.

Laurie: Another thing that people don't learn is that emotions are temporary and if we do appropriate things about them, then they go away and make space for the next emotion to come up.

But if we insist on hanging onto something, we can keep it around forever. I can find a way to stay angry for a very long time if I put my mind to it.

Interviewer: That sounds like work.

Laurie: It is. It is.

Jonathan: Actually, it's pretty easily automated. It's hard to outsource, but it can very easily be automated.

Interviewer: Interesting, but it's a strategy, just like not hanging onto the anger is a strategy.

Jonathan: Yes.

Laurie: Yes, and it's also a skill set because … We came up with a wonderful example. We need to do it for you.

Jonathan: Okay.

Laurie: This is the one that doesn't work and you could tell. I would say, and I do say, "You should pay this bill right away."

Jonathan: "I'm busy. Why are you always expecting me to do something different? You make me feel like whatever I do is wrong."

Laurie: Now that's a real example. That has happened, but this is how we do it now. "You should pay this bill right now."

Jonathan: "You mean for me to drop what I'm doing and handle it immediately?"

Laurie: "No, I really mean that you get it done before the end of the day."

Jonathan: "Why is it important to get it done by then?"

Laurie: "Well, she's a small vendor and she told me she needs the money as quickly as possible."

Jonathan: "Well, she's not going to get it any sooner if I do it before the end of the day. How about if I make sure it gets out in tomorrow's mail?"

Laurie: "That'll work."

Jonathan: "Okay."

Laurie: See, it takes a little longer, but we're both taking responsibility for pushing for what we want.

Interviewer: Okay, and that again, it just also sounds like something that you need to practice and communicate and just keep working at it.

Laurie: Over and over and over again. I mean, we've been doing it for 50 years, Jim, and it just ... We still have to do it.

Interviewer: Right.

Jonathan: Yes, it doesn't become automatic and solved once and for all so it has to be handled every time it comes up and it will come up frequently.

Interviewer: Excellent, so it sounds like you got to make a choice to do it too.

Jonathan: Yes, deliberate choice.

Interviewer: Okay, excellent. Anything else about my partner is responsible for how I feel?

Laurie: I would say if there's an argument that keeps going around in circles and doesn't go anywhere, suspect that that's what's going on.

Interviewer: Okay, all right. Excellent, and so you have a recurring pattern over and over, there's something else going on there that you should address.

Jonathan: Yes, the recurring things are generally about the same content over and over again. And whatever this is, it's not about the content. It's about how you're dealing with each other.

Interviewer: Okay, kind of the rules that you have set up between you, either on purpose or by de facto?

Jonathan: Yes, I think one of the unconscious rules, and maybe it'll show up in one of the other things, is that we're in a contest and one of us is going to win and the other one's going to lose.

Laurie: I think that's the next point.

Interviewer: Let's move on to the next point.

Chapter 9:
We Shouldn't Argue

Interviewer: Hidden beliefs about relationship number nine:

I shouldn't argue with my husband or wife.

Now, I guess one of the first things you should do is kind of define the word argue and then what should people do instead and why?

Jonathan: I think part of this is that people confuse disagreements and differences with arguments.

They think if there's a difference or a disagreement that means there's an argument or there's going to be an argument, so we have to bury those.

In this one, unlike the previous one where somebody may not be aware of their belief, usually somebody's quite aware that there is something going on here.

They're aware that there is a problem, but they have the belief that they can't stand conflict or that their partner can't stand conflict.

It's often a residue from bad experiences in childhood dealing with conflicts where they don't get resolved. They just make people feel bad and then get buried.

Laurie: The thing that people really need to learn is that conflict is inevitable and it doesn't necessarily have to be destructive.

But if people are afraid of conflict they've probably not developed negotiation skills or it hasn't occurred to them that they can use negotiation skills in private life.

I've often had people who are very skilled negotiators in business and it didn't occur to them that they could take it into their relationship and use that same skill there.

Interviewer: Do you have any resources or anything on your websites or anything you could point people to for learning these types of skills because I think this is critical that people understand that conflict and disagreement does not have to turn into a knock-down, drag-out argument fight.

Laurie: The Being Happy book (*Being Happy Together: How to Have a Fabulous Relationship with Your Life Partner in Less Than an Hour a Week*), which is really a program, has got a ton of things, actually 125 different things that people can negotiate about.

There are specific ideas about how to do it, how to say things about it and why to say certain things about it.

Jonathan: There are also, on one of our other websites, our main brochure site which is www.empowermentsystems.com, there's a link to some handouts with some articles specifically about conflict. We've had that up for a long time.

Interviewer: Okay. People can check out those two, but definitely this is an area at least in my own personal life, where I had to train my wife how to not lock down and close up.

But then, that was something that was learned from her parents which was learned from their parents.

Jonathan: There's also a really good book. It's not one of ours, but I want to just mention it. It's called the *Magic of Conflict* by Tom Crum. He's an Aikido master and it's a very interesting book about how conflict doesn't mean contest.

It's an opportunity to figure out how to resolve things when two people want something different at the same time—which happens all the time.

Interviewer: You mentioned that earlier, that you don't want to get in a situation where it's a contest between you and your spouse. Elaborate on that if you don't mind.

Jonathan: It's a fairly pervasive belief system, I think, in our culture. I'm not sure about other cultures, but certainly Western cultures.

It's that if I want something and you want something different then what this is about is who is going to win. All kinds of things follow from the point of view that it's a contest that you either win or lose.

One of the things that follows is that somebody winds up being a loser and then tries to get back. We develop whole sets of strategies about

* How to not lose, or

* How to win, or

* How to not give an advantage to the other person, or

* How to get back if we lost the last round.

There's a whole arena that doesn't have to happen if you re-frame it as "this isn't a contest." We just both want different things. Let's figure out how to produce it.

Laurie: One of the things that people very often get into extreme contests about is how to do something to achieve the same end that they both want.

They keep arguing for what is it that they want without ever talking about the reasons that they think what they want will work. We need to train people to talk about reasons instead of outcomes.

To set an outcome and then talk about possibilities. We often do that.

It just occurred to me that there is another resource that we have. That is the LaurieWeiss.com site.

We have a lot of websites, but there's a whole paper about "care-frontation" rather than confrontation that might be helpful to people.

Interviewer: Excellent and what was that website again?

Laurie: www.LaurieWeiss.com

Interviewer: Excellent. Anything else about argument between husbands and wives that is critical to know?

Laurie: I think we've done it pretty well.

Jonathan: Yes.

Chapter 10:
Two Become One

Interviewer: We've made it to hidden belief number ten.

Jonathan: Woohoo.

Laurie: Wow.

Interviewer: Hidden beliefs about relationships number ten:

Either you have to give up yourself to be in a marriage or you have to give up the marriage in order to be yourself.

I've heard this one in the past. What exactly is this mistake and what should people do instead to hang onto their self and to keep the marriage strong and happy as well.

Laurie: It's a common belief in our culture that when two people get married, two become one, but what that really means is that each one has to give up half of themselves in order to make a complete marriage.

Jonathan: Or to make the math work, two half people equal one marriage.

Laurie: The problem is that what do you do with the other half? Especially since probably it was the other half that attracted your spouse in the first place.

Jonathan: By the way, it doesn't work any better if one is three-fourths and the other is one fourth, to add up to one whole. Both need to be whole people.

Interviewer: That makes a lot of sense. What are some strategies to make sure you hang onto the whole you and get the marriage right as well?

Laurie: First of all, the thing to know is that everybody puts their best face forward during a courtship. Everybody hides the things they think that their partner won't like, and it's universal. You can't not do it. It happens.

Then those hidden things start showing up. When they show up, it's like my mother told me that I should do everything the way my husband wanted me to.

It's a horrible thing to do because one of the ways it showed up is that I was supposed to give up the classical music that I love and start liking jazz which he loved.

I did that for about a year or so or maybe two years. Then he hauled me into a therapist because we were growing apart so much that we were unhappy with each other.

The therapist told me it's okay to like classical music. It's okay to go see the opera if you want to.

What we tell people to do instead is show those things a little bit at a time, talk about them, negotiate about them, figure out how they're going to fit into the relationship and if they don't fit into the relationship, to not give them up anyway.

Jonathan: One of the assumptions that keeps this in place is that now that we're married we have to do everything together. We're not entitled to any private time or space or private life now that we're married. That's not really valid.

We each need our own privacy, our own energy and stuff like that that has nothing to do with our partner. We're complete people aside from the relationship.

We need some place to express that, whether it's our hobbies or things that we like to spend time doing that the other has no interest or energy for. We need to negotiate ways to make time and space for those things.

Interviewer: How would you do that? How would you come to that negotiation?

Laurie: You would say, "I saw this thing advertised in the newspaper that I would really like to do."

Jonathan: I think it would be a waste of time and money for me to do this with you because I wouldn't get anything out of it. Can you find someone else to go with or are you okay with going by yourself?

Interviewer: Then that brings us back to either hidden belief number 8 or hidden belief number 9 or hidden belief number 7.

Laurie: Right. Package.

Interviewer: You get into a situation where "If you loved me you'd go." So what do you do?

Laurie: In some sense that's true. Sometimes it is. I would really, really, really like you to come.

It's really important that there's somebody else there with me that I can count on to support me, even if you don't want to be there. Come anyway.

Jonathan: Yes. That frees me to decide supporting her is important, and this isn't going to hurt me or harm me. I may not get the value out of it that she is, but if that's important to her, I'll support it. Okay.

Interviewer: It puts a different reason why you're there. You're not there because you're forced to be. You're there because you love your wife and you want to hang out with her.

Jonathan: It's a choice. There was an instance some years ago where somebody came through town doing a genealogy of Laurie's family and invited her to come out to the airport to be interviewed. He was just passing through town.

She wanted me to come with her. I haven't got the slightest interest in genealogy and certainly not of her family, but it was important to her.

I just thought, "Well what the heck. I'll just support it." I came and I found a corner to read a book, and it worked for both of us.

Interviewer: That sounds really good. You got to be you and you got to work on the marriage. This one actually it seems like it really pulls together the other nine beliefs.

Jonathan: Yes. There's a line that we're fond of from "My Fair Lady":

"Rather than do either we do something else that neither likes at all." That's not what we mean by working it together.

Interviewer: There you go. Anything else on this last belief or should we move on to the conclusion?

Jonathan: Just mentioning the costs of hanging on to this belief which is pretty high.

Interviewer: In what way?

Jonathan: Very often what will happen if you hide part of yourself is that it doesn't go away so you go out and find someone else who will appreciate it.

You wind up hanging out with them because they appreciate a part of you you've never shown your partner or the partner's never seen.

Interviewer: Wow. Yes. I can see that. I can really see that. Excellent. Let's keep going.

Chapter 11:
It Should be Easy

Interviewer: As we bring this into conclusion, is there anything else we need to know about this book project?

Laurie: I think the very important thing about this is it's a beginning. There is something else that is important, though.

It's that a long time ago we made a commitment to support each other's growth and development even if it put the relationship at risk.

Interviewer: What do you mean by that?

Laurie: It means that we had each had the experience of being very, very strongly drawn to something that has taken us away from the other for a period of time.

We wanted to learn something. We wanted to do something. The commitment is to go ahead and do it, that the other one will support it, and will keep the home fires burning.

We do very intense things. Jonathan went to Australia for six weeks, eight weeks, to learn how to do something that he thought he might like in order to take his career in that direction.

Since we had been working together for a long time that was a very risky thing for me to say "Okay, go ahead and do it."

By the time we got back together I wasn't even sure that I wanted to stay married to him, because he'd left me at a really vulnerable time.

But we had that commitment and we worked through it. Those kinds of things have come up over and over again.

Jonathan: In both directions. When one of us is really drawn to something that means there's growth for us and there's benefits to the other for each of us to grow. We recognized that early on and decided to commit to supporting it.

Interviewer: That makes a lot of sense, but that also takes some guts.

Laurie: It does, but having a relationship that you want to grow and be everything that it can be takes guts. There's no way around it.

It takes giving up beliefs that you've held dear for a long time. It takes a commitment to grow up.

Jonathan: Apparently it works, and we're celebrating our 50th anniversary.

Interviewer: You think it will work out?

Jonathan: So far.

Laurie: It might.

Interviewer: If you keep working at it.

Jonathan: Yes.

Laurie: Uh huh.

Interviewer: What should people's number one takeaway be from our session today, besides that you've got to make that commitment? What else should a big takeaway be?

Laurie: That you can have a great relationship, but it does take conscious attention and deliberate practice. It's not going to happen unless you commit to doing it.

Interviewer: That makes a lot of sense. Are there any additional resources that people should know about? You've mentioned several of your websites.

Why don't you just recap those or any other resources people should really know about and take advantage of.

Laurie: The first one is at www.beinghappybook.com. That is a program called *Being Happy Together: How to Create a Fabulous Relationship with Your Life Partner in Less Than an Hour a Week.*

Another resource on conflict is at www.empowerment systems.com. One on confrontation, "Care-frontation" is at www.laurieweiss.com.

Jonathan: We also have a site where some of this is applied to business communication and relationships. That's at www.daretosayit.com.

Interviewer: Excellent. As we bring this into conclusion, what's the number one action item people should take as a result of this audiobook? Listening to their spouse?

Jonathan: Talk and listen. Talk about what's going on inside. Listen to what the other person's saying.

Sometimes we have to literally tie people down and make them listen, but once we get the hang of it it's not so hard.

Laurie: Listening is a real skill. Sometimes people say "Uh huh," thinking that they've heard, but if you ask them to repeat it back, they didn't get what was really meant.

Sometimes we teach people to listen by having them just sit and repeat back what they think they've heard until the other person says "Yes, you've got it."

Jonathan: That's what it was.

Laurie: Then they switch. Listening is the most important thing that people can do. It's the greatest gift you can give to anybody else.

Interviewer: Excellent. I want to thank you both for what's been a very, very informative and educational time together. I would encourage everyone to go check out the resources, URLs that have been shared.

This has been the *Top Ten Hidden Beliefs About Relationships and How to Stop Them from Poisoning Your Marriage*, with Doctors Laurie Weiss and Jonathan Weiss. Everyone have a great day, and thanks for joining us.

Reminder

Claim Your Gift Here

If you have not claimed your gift yet, do it now.

A VERY SPECIAL 60 MINUTE RECORDING

Our conversation with a group of lay
marriage counselors.

Little Known Secrets of Relationship Development
(MP3 Audio)

When you understand that relationships move through a
normal cycle of development, you are less likely to worry
about the natural and healthy changes you experience in
your marriage.

http://tinyurl.com/5cpqb4

Please Help Me Reach New Readers

I hope you enjoyed **Stop Poisoning Your Marriage with These Common Beliefs**. I have to tell you when we originally recorded this material, I did not know it would become a book. Some of my clients found the material so valuable that they urged me to make it available this way.

Chances are that you checked out the reviews on this book when you purchased it. Reviews are critical to help prospective readers decide to read books. I would be thrilled if you would leave a review NOW, while you are thinking about it.

If you are someone who has done this before, you know how easy it is.

If you're not, you may be shuddering at the memory of grade school book reviews. This is different!!! Really it is!

All you need to do is imagine that you are telling a friend about reading this book. Then follow these steps.

- Say what you would tell your friend into your phone and record it in the notes section and let your phone write it out. (All you need to say is one or two sentences.)

- Email it to yourself.

- Add punctuation if necessary.

- Cut and paste your sentences into a review box wherever you buy your books.

I have included a few links to popular places to leave your reviews. Go to www.BooksbyLaurie.com or www.Good reads.com/Laurie_Weiss and click on any book title. Scroll down to find the instructions to leave a review.

I would love to hear from you about how this book impacted you. And, if you have any problems or questions about this book I would really appreciate hearing from you directly. My email address is Laurie@LaurieWeiss.com. You will find my phone number and social media connections on another page.

Thank you in advance for taking the time to contribute to the conversation about what to read. I truly appreciate it.

Laurie

P.S. PLEASE take a few minutes to leave that review now, before life gets in your way.

P.P.S. When you read my author bio at www.Booksby Laurie.com you will find several free gifts you may enjoy.

Acknowledgments

Without Jim Edwards this project would not have happened at all. He offered to interview us and created the original Audio Book CD, *The Top 10 Hidden Beliefs about Relationships and How to Stop Them from Poisoning Your Marriage* by Laurie Weiss Ph.D. and Jonathan B. Weiss Ph.D. (Audio CD - Feb 7, 2011). This is available only from Amazon.com.

Jim is a prolific writer and public figure. www.facebook.com/TheNetReporter. Thank you, Jim!

About the Author

Relationship Communication Experts, Dr. Laurie Weiss and Dr. Jonathan Weiss are internationally known as experts who help other relationship consultation professionals develop their skills.

As psychotherapists, coaches, marriage counselors, authors and stress-relief experts they have helped more than 60,000 individuals reclaim life energy and find joy in life for more than four decades. They have taught professionals in 13 countries and Dr. Laurie has authored eight books that make complex information accessible to anyone. Her latest, *Letting It Go*, teaches rapid anxiety and stress relief. www.LaurieWeiss.com

Currently, they are the only two Master Certified Logosynthesis Practitioners in the United States. They are Certified Transactional Analysis Trainers with Clinical Specialties. Dr Laurie also has an Organizational Specialty and is a Master Certified Coach. Her work has been translated into German, Chinese, Spanish, French and Portuguese.

She is passionate about helping people have the important conversations that build great personal and working relationships. She says, "I have an unshakeable belief, based on over 45 years of experience, that people are doing the very best they can with the resources they have available to them at any given moment."

Married in 1960, they started working together in 1970. Both Drs. Weiss love mixing business and pleasure and enjoy visiting professional colleagues and friends around the globe. They live and work in Littleton, CO, USA.

E-mail: Dr. Laurie at Laurie@LaurieWeiss.com and Dr. Jonathan at Weiss@EmpowermentSystems.com

Office: 303-794-5379

How to Work with
Dr. Laurie or Dr. Jonathan

We have been married since 1960 and business partners since 1972 when we were teaching Transactional Analysis throughout the United States. We have been learning and teaching cutting edge tools for healing and transformation for over 45 years.

We have both been Teaching and Supervising Transactional Analysts for over four decades. Currently we are the only Certified Logosynthesis Practitioners in the United States. Either or both of us would be delighted to help you learn more about creating joy and satisfaction in your life and your important relationships.

Contact Us: We Usually Answer the Phone

You can contact us directly to discuss what is best for you and your group. We offer a variety of options including CLASSES, TALKS, BOOK GROUP VISITS, PROFESSIONAL CONFERENCE PRESENTATIONS, TRAINING, INDIVIDUAL and COUPLES APPOINTMENTS. We work with our clients in person, by phone and by Skype.

Dr. Laurie Weiss:

LaurieWeiss@EmpowermentSystems.com

Dr. Jonathan Weiss: Weiss@EmpowermentSystems.com

Empowerment Systems

506 West Davies Way

Littleton, CO 80120 USA

303-794-5379

Websites

Personal: http://www.LaurieWeiss.com

Logosynthesis: http://www.LogosynthesisColorado.com

Business: http://www.EmpowermentSystems.com

Purchase Books: http://www.BooksbyLaurie.com

Social Media

Facebook: https://www.Facebook.com/laurieweiss

LinkedIn: http://www.LinkedIn.com/in/laurieweiss

Pinterest: https://www.Pinterest.com/laurieweiss/

Twitter: https://Twitter.com/@LaurieWeiss

Goodreads: https://www.Goodreads.com/Laurie_Weiss

Blogs

Personal Development:
http://www.IDontNeedTherapy.com/blog

Relationship: http://RelationshipHQ.com/blog/

Business Communication:
http://www.DareToSayIt.com/blog

About the Secrets of
Happy Relationships Series

Relationships aren't easy. Relationships are often confused and messy with partners trying to find happiness in all the wrong ways.

Real relationships get messy because even though you think your life partner is just like you, he or she isn't. You are two different people trying to meet the challenge of creating and maintaining a happy and loving relationship, perhaps without much useful information.

To make matters worse, you live in the midst of the outmoded role expectations of a culture that values drama and competition and extreme busyness. Most media doesn't help. It focuses on difficult relationships, not successful ones.

Ordinary relationships have their ups and downs and almost nobody writes about those cycles. It's no wonder there are so many misunderstandings. Creating a lasting, loving, growing relationship is an incredible challenge. It's completely natural to have questions about your relationship.

I've been answering questions about relationships since 1973 when I was in newly minted TA (Transactional Analysis) therapist and was sure I had the answers to all the problems of the world. I had been married for 13 years and we had survived some major challenges. I was happily learning and using our new tools. Over four decades later, we are still married and I've learned a lot.

It's been my pleasure and privilege to help people sort out the misconceptions, misunderstandings and challenges of creating happy, loving relationships. Being happy together is a gift my husband and I have given each other through the work of addressing issues as they arise. It's a gift you can have also; by giving it to each other.

Books in the Secrets of
Happy Relationships Series

Are You My Perfect Partner?
To Marry or Not to Marry ...
Are you really ready to get married?

Being Married:
Secrets Women Wish They Knew
Crucial information you need
to know about marriage

Stop Poisoning Your Marriage
with These Common Beliefs
Are you letting these myths
undermine your marriage?

Relationship Tips for Life Partners
Critical guidelines for creating a true partnership

Reconnect to Rescue Your Marriage:
Avoid Divorce and Feel Loved Again
What to do before leaving your troubled marriage

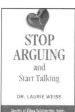

Stop Arguing and Start Talking …
even if you are afraid your only answer is divorce!
Are you ready to have these loving,
productive conversations with your spouse?

Being Happy Together:
What to Do to Keep Love Alive
Unlock secrets to rapid relationship
renewal in just an hour a week

Other Books by Laurie Weiss

**Letting It Go: Relieve Anxiety and Toxic
Stress in Just a Few Minutes Using Only Words
(Rapid Relief with Logosynthesis®)**
*Are you ready for relaxation to replace
anxiety in your life?*

**Emotional Self-Help: I Don't Need Therapy,
But Where Do I Turn for Answers?**
Do you need to become emotionally literate?
www.BooksByLaurie.com/answers

**Recovery From CoDependency:
It's Never Too Late To Reclaim Your Childhood**
Are you ready to release your codependency?
www.BooksByLaurie.com/recovery

An Action Plan for Your Inner Child:
Parenting Each Other
Are you ready to reclaim your inner child?
https://www.amazon.com/dp/1558741658

What Is the Emperor Wearing?
Truth-Telling in Business Relationships
Do you wish you dared to tell the truth?
www.BooksByLaurie.com/emperor

Enjoy this preview of another book in the
Secrets of Happy Relationships series:

Relationship Tips for Life Partners

Great relationships are not made in heaven. They do NOT require a soul mate, do not need to end when you fall out of love, are not always exciting, and are not limited to a few lucky people.

Great relationships do require information, attention, time and commitment to the challenge of creating them.

After many years as a relationship coach and marriage counselor, studying, practicing and teaching relationship building, I wrote down the tips I repeatedly give my clients.

Here is one useful tip from each section of the popular book that was originally published as *124 Tips for Having a Great Relationship*.

1. About Relationships

Expect the closeness and distance you experience with your partner to vary from hour to hour, day to day, and season to season. People experience enough closeness much as they experience enough food—any more leads to discomfort. We all have different capacities.

2. Communication

Say "Maybe" when you are not sure about something. Give a time when you will provide an answer and keep your commitment.

3. Difficult Communication

Speak in sentences or, at most, paragraphs instead of pages during a difficult conversation. Your partner will only remember the last sentence or two you say and forget the beginning of a long speech.

4. Play

Laugh together. Share the jokes or cartoons that make you grin, rent a funny video, or remember the stories about funny things (especially in retrospect) you've experienced together.

5. Tasks

Hire someone to do the chores you both hate—or do them together. Start by looking at the things that never seem to get done, probably because neither of you wants to do them.

6. Boundaries

Name the movie *you* would like to see, or the restaurant *you* like best, before you ask your partner's preference. That way you avoid being angry because your partner did not read your mind.

7. Money

Create shared financial goals. Be sure you discuss and agree on priorities. If one of you thinks your savings are for a great vacation and the other expects to use them to invest for financial independence, you are headed for trouble.

8. Special Occasions

Give gifts that your partner has indicated that s/he wants or needs instead of what you believe s/he wants or needs. You can give other gifts, too, but first paying attention to your partner avoids disappointment.

9. Separateness

Encourage your partner to grow and develop in his/her own way. This does *not* mean to chase your spouse around the house with a self-help book.

10. Togetherness

Expect major life changes to impact your relationship. Having a baby, losing a job, getting a new job, illness, death of a parent, retirement, etc., may create a need to renegotiate almost everything you thought was settled.

11. Care of Your Partner

Hug your partner frequently—not just when you want to get sexy. Touch is an important way that people use to know that they are loved.

12. Self Care

Do whatever makes you feel vibrant and alive, even if you need to do it alone. When you feel vibrant and alive, you are attractive to your partner and to others.

* * *

You'll find links to all the *Secrets of Happy Relationship Series* books at www.BooksbyLaurie.com. Go there now and order the next book you need to create the happy relationship you want and deserve.

Made in the USA
Columbia, SC
11 October 2020

22612463R00059